How

Happy

A self-help guide for baffled gentlefolk

Geoff Hill

Geoff Hill: what the critics say

Geoff Hill has an outstanding writing talent with a wicked sense of fun. Brilliant writing, genuinely and originally funny, and a supremely entertaining read.

Martyn Lewis, broadcaster

He has wonderful views on life, a great turn of phrase and a great sense of humour. His off-beat observations and zany outlook on life are laugh-out-loud funny.

John Mullin, The Independent

Hill has a voice all his own - both lyrical and lunatic - which casts the world in a new light.

Mark Sanderson, Independent on Sunday

Hilarious.

Lois Rathbone, The Times

Geoff Hill is a comic genius. I laughed until I cried, my nose bled and I lost control of my bowels. I may well have to kill him when I meet him.

Patrick Taylor, author of New York Times bestseller An Irish Country Doctor

Brilliant. At times laugh-out-loud funny, and at others intensely moving, which is part of Geoff's genius. He's a writer for whom the words highly and recommended were invented.

Brian Page, Mensa magazine

A brilliant read.

Dave Myers, BBC's Hairy Biker

Prologue

Bertrand Russell once got into the back of a London cab, and after a few seconds of glancing at him in the rear view mirror, the driver turned around and said: "Here, you're Bertrand Russell the philosopher, innit?"

"Well, yes, I am," said Russell, delighted at having been recognised by a member of the hoi polloi.

"What's it all about, then, Bertrand?" said the driver.

Russell's reply is not recorded, but his later quote is: "The secret of happiness is to face the fact that life is horrible, horrible, horrible."

Honestly, Bertrand, is that the best you can come up with after a lifetime of thought?

Not that he was the only gloomy philosopher around. Although John Stuart Mill and Jeremy Bentham stuck their heads above the parapet in the 19th Century and declared that the goal of personal and political life should be happiness, it didn't do much good for either Bertrand or Ludwig Wittgenstein, who once muttered: "'I don't know why we are here, but I'm pretty sure that it is not in order to enjoy ourselves."

After losing the will to live struggling through his work at university, I can see what he means. No wonder he and Russell were soulmates, since at times only four students, one of them Wittgenstein, turned up for his lectures at Cambridge.

Stuff that, I say. No one wants to know that life is miserable. What they want to know is how to be happy.

Somebody really should write a book about it. So here goes.

Geoff Hill, December 2021

If you're unhappy and you know it, raise your hands

Hands up who wants to be happy. Hands up who wants to love and be loved.

Ah yes, all but one as usual. There's always a masochist down the back whose idea of happiness is a cold shower and a damned good thrashing. Just to remind them of public school.

For the rest of us, happiness and love are what we all want, but the ironic thing is that the more we desperately strive for both, the less likely we are to find them. Ask Woody Allen. Or Elizabeth Taylor. I can't believe why those two never hooked up. They were made for each other.

So stop struggling. Just follow a few simple rules, and happiness will follow. And once you are happy, love will follow too.

And simplicity is the key. A few years ago I interviewed the charming and charismatic Robin Sharma, the author of The Monk Who Sold His Ferrari, and bought his book The Greatness Guide.

It was full of great ideas for greatness, but by the time I'd got to number 4,587 I'd forgotten the first 4,586, and didn't feel so great.

Life's too short, and complexity is self-defeating, so keep it simple.

Before light, darkness. As they say in Tia Maria ads

Depression: the best thing that ever happened to me.

In 1994, I split up with my girlfriend of eight years, my sister died of cancer, my granny died of too many birthdays and my house renovations ran way over budget. Don't they all?

I stopped sleeping, had to quit work and ended up in a mental hospital, convinced that my life was over and that I would never work, love, enjoy anything or have any sort of normal life again. Suicide seemed the only answer.

When I recovered, mostly thanks to the love of family and friends, I knew three things.

That life would never be that bad again.

That every day is a blessing.

And from talking to people about my experience and finding out that many of them had been through the same thing, or knew someone who had, that we are all the same, and have the same hopes, fears and dreams.

That in itself is an antidote to the unhappiness of feeling alone in the world, and thinking that no one else is going through what we are.

We all are. Just talk, listen, and you'll find that out for yourself.

Auschwitz. The second best thing.

After a day walking around there, I thought: Problems? I don't have any problems compared to this. And any I think I have today, I look back to that day and think: well, it's not Auschwitz, and nobody's dead.

The lesson? Get some perspective. If you've got a roof over your head and food and drink on the table, you're doing OK. Everything else is a bonus. Even the drink is a bonus, although you try telling an Irishman that.

And if you think I don't know how bad it can get, here's the article I wrote after I recovered from depression in 1994, and a subsidiary article called The truth behind a monster. The response to it was incredible, from people who said they'd gone through the same thing, or knew a friend or relative who had, but had never talked about it because of the perceived stigma.

One step from death

I sat on the edge of the bed in the mental hospital, my head in my hands and my life over.

"There is no hope. I can see no way out," I said to myself.

Then I lifted my head and saw the way out.

Chris, the manic depressive in the next bed, had left his Ribena bottle behind.

He had spent the entire night muttering to himself, placing all his possessions on the bed, packing them away then starting all over again.

The bottle he had left behind was made of glass. If I broke it I could cut my wrists and free myself from the endless days and sleepless nights of torture which had become my life.

"Do it," said a voice inside my head. "Do it and get it over with."

I got up and started to walk towards the bottle, and at that moment a nurse walked through the door with a bunch of flowers.

"For you, from friends in London," she said.

Those flowers saved my life.

My journey to hell began with the death of my sister Shirley from cancer. Even now I don't know which is worse, watching someone you love suffer, or being with them when they die.

Then my girlfriend and I split up after living together for eight years. Although we had both met other people and agreed to separate and stay the best of friends, the sight of her packing her clothes, her books and her plants into boxes and moving out was like someone taking a blunt knife to my heart.

For weeks afterwards I came home to the house from work, looked around at the empty spaces and felt as if in a short time I had become a lonely old man who had crossed the border into an East German of the soul, without life, light, flowers or colour.

Then my grandmother died, the volleyball team I coach broke up in a not particularly pleasant way, the renovations to the house cost a third more than I'd estimated, and my new girlfriend in England left for a nine-month trip around the world which she'd planned before we met.

I was left alone with the thoughts inside my head. For a while I did all the right things. I looked after myself, had dinner parties so the house was often full of people, read books like Louise Hay's You Can Heal Your Life, and went to see a counsellor called Michelle Toner, who helped me discover that I had great trouble letting go of the past before I felt I could get on with the future.

Now, you'd think that since I'd written two novels about men who were desperately trying to let go of the past so they could love and be loved in the future, I'd realise that was the problem in my own life. You'd think so, but novelists are obviously just as stupid as anyone else.

Or maybe they just need the past more than other people. After all, Ernest Hemingway had electric shock treatment for mental illness, but when the treatment also wiped out his memories, he killed himself. Without his past, the narrative source of all his writing and his ability to make connections was gone, and with it the point of his life.

Christmas came closer. Behind every corner, memory waited to pounce. In the back yard, the yellow frame of my ex-girlfriend's bicycle glowed like a lantern down all the dark days, simultaneously taunting and comforting. The sound of children singing Silent Night was enough to reduce me to tears.

I spent hours on end trying to decide what I was going to do over Christmas. Being with my family would be unbearably sad after the death of my sister, being with my ex-girlfriend's family would be impossible because I was missing her so much, and going to see my new girlfriend in Bali could be a disaster because I was missing my ex so much.

I thought about it, and thought about it. Finally the triangle of tension tightened so much that I stopped sleeping, and when I weighed myself one morning, found to my surprise that I'd lost almost two stone.

That weekend, I went to a volleyball tournament in Enniskillen that I'd always gone to with my ex, and on the Sunday night, exhausted by lack of sleep, constant worrying and the stress of playing and coaching the new team I'd joined, arrived home on the Sunday night to an empty house, burst into tears and realised that I couldn't take it any more.

My old friend Gerry called to ask if I was OK.

"I just don't know what to do," I sobbed.

The next day, he drove me to see my doctor, and when I told him I was having suicidal thoughts, he said I needed to be in Windsor House, the psychiatric unit of Belfast City Hospital.

I checked in that afternoon, and explained the background to the resident psychiatrist. That was the last I was to see of her for two days.

Windsor House is a dreadful place. When you walk through the doors, you feel as if you have stepped into a Victorian lunatic asylum.

Even sane visitors were disturbed by its clinical, institutional atmosphere, and every ex-patient I have spoken to since then has roundly condemned it.

I entered the place in terror and turmoil, my mind swinging wildly from suicidal panic to inexplicable euphoria, and found nothing there to take my mind off that turmoil.

The games room consisted of a box of Trivial Pursuit, and most of the patients spent their days sitting on their beds staring into space, wandering endlessly up and down the corridor, sitting in a smoke-filled room looking at the walls or watching soap operas on television.

Although the nurses were pleasant and willing to listen, not one of them told me what was happening to me. But when you are utterly convinced that there is no point going on with your life, the only thing that keeps you alive is the knowledge, either from those who have been there or those who deal with it professionally, that other people have been there and survived.

On the second dreadful afternoon I found a book on cognitive therapy on the floor of one of the day rooms, and filled in a questionnaire in it which finally told me that what I was apparently suffering from was severe clinical depression.

I sat all day with the book, exhausted through lack of sleep and trying to work through the exercises in it. Finally, I went to bed at 1am, hearing imaginary conversations in my head, and slept for an hour.

I lay there for the rest of the night, feeling as if the clutch had gone in my head, so that no matter how much my mind raced it couldn't move my life forward.

The next morning, even the decision to get up for breakfast filled me with terror. I paced the corridors endlessly, trying to tire myself out enough to go back to sleep.

After an hour, a nurse took me to to see the resident psychiatrist, who was wearing a dark green knitted suit with suspiciously flared trousers.

"What can I do for you, Mr Hill?" she said coolly.

"Well, I know the NHS is understaffed and facing financial problems, but this place is completely non-conducive to mental health and is making me worse rather than better. If you weren't mad when you came in, you'd end up that way pretty quickly," I said.

"Also, I've come in here in a state which is completely terrifying, and yet the only people who've told me what's happening to me are my mother and Carine Minne, a psychiatrist I know in London, on the phone.

"Both of them told me that I was suffering the symptoms of severe depression, that I would continue to have waves of panic attacks and suicidal feelings over the next few weeks, and that my only objective was to do nothing except stay safe and get through these, for in time they would ease, the good bits would get longer, and eventually the panic would go away and I would get better.

"Knowing that has kept me alive, and yet I got none of this advice from inside the hospital."

"We're just observing your sleeping and eating patterns at the moment to see if you are actually depressed," she said.

"But I found out I was severely depressed by doing the questionnaire in this book, and you don't need to see whether I have Irish stew or chicken casserole to find out whether I'm depressed or not."

"I accept your point that things in here could be better, but it will take time. We'll have to observe you for up to a week, and then you might be able to get half an hour's counselling twice a week," she said.

I didn't think my heart could sink any further, but it did.

At lunchtime, Tony, a small, nervous ex-boxer from Belfast, was having a panic attack, raising his spoon to his mouth over and over again without putting any food in. The staff were elsewhere, filling in forms and handing out food.

Raymond, a man from the Shankill Road who'd been caught in the 1993 fishmonger's bombing and kept getting terrifying flashbacks, sat down beside him.

"Tony, name me the current heavyweight champion."

Tony stopped. "George Foreman," he said.

"And the one before that."

Tony started talking, and eating. Half an hour later he had finished his food and was walking down the corridor muttering "Rocky Marciano" to himself over and over again.

I went and sat in the day room with Raymond.

"I think we're the only two sane people in the place," he said.

Five minutes later a blonde woman came in and sat across the room staring at me, her foot swinging to and fro.

"Are you married?" she said.

"Afraid not," I said.

"I'm from Helen's Bay," she said. "Would you like to give me a kiss?"

That afternoon, I checked out, walked nervously through the doors and went to stay with my sister's family in Newtownards. That night, in a room lined with Thomas the Tank Engine wallpaper, I had my first night's sleep in weeks, if not months. Before I slept, I felt as if I heard ravens in tall trees, and imagined that it was the madness escaping.

But the next day, I woke in a cold sweat, terrified at the thought of getting out of bed and facing the day. I lay in bed until dark, shaking.

"I don't know what to do," I told my mother when she called around.

"Come walking," she said.

We went out into a biting wind, under a cruel sky. Above our heads, clouds devoured the frightened stars as my mother talked of us as children, walking on Saturdays to Betty Cowan's to wash a week's dishes and help with the hay for a reward of tea and boiled eggs.

I could not remember, but was glad of a past when the world was young, before all this had begun.

And then she told me that in those days, depression had overtaken her too, and she had overcome it on her own. I found it almost impossible to imagine how.

"I just feel sure that my life has fallen completely to pieces, and I'll never put them back together again. Sure that I'll never have a happy, normal life again. That I'll never write or play sport or go back to work or fall in love, or ever find any joy in anything again," I said.

"That's exactly the way you do feel. But you will get better. You'll look back on this as the worst time in your life, and be a stronger, wiser person because you got through it and will never be this bad again. I promise you that, and I wouldn't lie to you," she said.

"I know," I said nervously, wondering if she was telling the truth or just saying that to make me feel better.

And so the endless days began, each of them a journey from madness to strength.

Every morning I woke and lay for hours in terror, my mind and heart racing and my foot tapping endlessly against the bottom of the bed. Thoughts raced through my head, simultaneously crucial and irrelevant. Occasionally I shook from head to foot with muscular spasms. The thought of getting up, having a shower and getting dressed filled me with panic.

At times the conviction that there was no way out except death came back. At six one morning, after a sleepless night, I lay looking at the plug on the wall. If I stuck my fingers down the back of it and held the bedframe with my other hand, it would make a circuit through my lost heart. Do it, I thought.

God knows what held me back. Some tiny, unspoken hope that people were telling the truth when they said I would get out of this.

On Tuesday December 12, I was supposed to meet my ex to discuss things. The night before, I sat down in my Thomas the Tank Engine room and began calmly to plan my suicide if she said it was finally over between us.

I would drive my car up to Shaw's Bridge, drink a last Black Bush, take some sleeping tablets, then pass a hosepipe from the exhaust through the barely open window and fall asleep one last time listening to Rachmaninov's Second Piano Concerto.

I would leave behind a note apologising to all and blaming no one, and asking for my ashes to be scattered on the sea beside a log cabin in Finland where in 1984 I had spent the happiest days of my life.

I was writing out the inscription for the plaque to be mounted on a rock by the shore when the phone rang. It was Carine, the psychiatrist in London who had sent me the flowers.

I told her calmly what I was doing.

"Listen, do something for me. Give your car keys to your sister, and put off the meeting with your ex until you can cope with whatever the outcome is. Will you do that for me?" she said.

What she said was entirely reasonable, although at the time I thought she was over-reacting a little.

After all, I was only being rational in planning my death because there was no point in life.

And then, at the other end of the scale, there were evenings of euphoria when I felt I could deal with anything; as if I could go back to work, to life. As if I could read a book, listen to a record, fall in love. But then I realised that I was describing was the bliss of normality, of everyday life.

And bliss it was. The joy I felt the first evening I was able to sit down and enjoy some music was so indescribable that I cried.

But the bad days returned, snapping at my heels like wounded hounds. Christmas Day came and went, a dim lantern in the dark.

Friends called around, saving me with their love. When you are sure that you are alone, sometimes all you need to prove you wrong is a hug.

I signed up for practical philosophy and art classes, and began to meditate, to connect with my senses, to live from day to day, to stop regretting the past and worrying about the future.

And I began to realise that I should learn to enjoy things as they are, rather than always trying to make them perfect and just ending up frustrated.

To realise that not all problems can be solved by thinking about them, and that some have to be left to solve themselves through stillness and acceptance.

That a mind which can be still can produce more wisdom than a mind in constant movement.

I had suffered so much pain that at times ordinary life became an astonishing experience. When those times came I felt like a child, filled with wonder and curiosity at the simplest of things, like walking in the rain, sunlight on brick, or the simplicity of bread and wine.

The bad days came back, but I was still and let them pass.

And now I know at last that one day, before sooner becomes later, I will finally reach the edge of the black pit, haul myself over the precipice and see, glittering in the sunshine, a land of lakes and forests, rivers and mountains, which I thought I would never see again.

A land called the future.

The truth behind a monster

Depression can affect anyone, no matter how rich, successful or apparently happy they are.

I lost count of the people who said to me: "You're the last person I would have expected to suffer from depression."

The official figures are that one in four people suffer from it at some stage, and it is twice as common in women as in men. I suspect the true figures are much higher, since people don't talk about it because of the stigma attached.

Symptoms include apathy, lack of motivation, trouble sleeping, loss of self-esteem and feelings of utter helplessness.

Some people react by losing their appetite and weight, others by nibbling at food constantly and putting on weight. Other physical symptoms include headaches and digestive problems.

The wild mood swings I experienced, from complete terror first thing in the morning to euphoria late at night, are common. As a general rule, they tend to flatten out, and then the good spells become the norm rather than the exception.

Bad days can recur for months, but when they disappear you will enjoy life more than ever. Take my word for it. I'm now more happy, content and relaxed than I've ever been.

Depression has various causes. Freudians believe that the roots are formed in childhood, when we suffer traumatic losses like the end of breastfeeding, leaving us with frustration and anger in adulthood.

It can also run in families. My sister and mother both suffered, for example.

Chemical imbalances in the brain can also be a reason, and several antidepressants such as Prozac indirectly increase the level of serotonin, which is normally low in depressed people.

A change in lifestyle, or traumatic events like bereavement, relationship difficulties, unemployment, physical illness or stress can also cause it. So can certain times of life, like after giving birth, middle age or growing old.

You can cope by yourself, although if you are feeling suicidal or close to it, you must be safe and among people.

When you get over the feeling that the only way out is to kill yourself, there are things you can do to help, although being with people is still a good idea. Even talking to them about how bad your feelings are will help.

Other good things to do are:

- Look after yourself. Eat good, simple food, get plenty of sleep, don't drink too much and give yourself regular treats to look forward to.

- If you can, get up as soon as you wake up. The longer you stay in bed, the worse you feel and the harder it is to get up. Even the act of getting up can give you enough of a sense of achievement to get you through the worst part of the day.

- Do one thing at a time, give it your full attention while you're doing it, and pause briefly before you go on to something else. If you are running around the kitchen and feel hungry, for example, sit down and relax before you eat.

- Plan your day so that you only do the amount of things you feel comfortable with. On my worst days, the only thing I was capable of was getting out of bed and getting dressed, but once I did that I was often able to go for a walk, and felt better for it. Gentle physical exercise like walking, cycling and swimming are all good, especially in the fresh air, if only because they help you sleep.

- Live in the moment. I spent years ruining today by comparing it with yesterday and wondering how it would compare with tomorrow. Now I just enjoy it.

- Connect with your senses. Sit down twice a day and feel the weight of your body on the chair, the air on your skin, the smells in your nose, the taste in your mouth. Pick an object and look at it, or close your eyes and listen to the most distant sounds you can. If thoughts come into your head, don't fight them. Just let them pass away like a river. This is an exercise close to meditation, and has the same purpose; to help you still your mind.

- Try relaxation or stress management classes.

- Take up a new hobby.

I can also recommend several books:

Overcoming Depression by Dr Caroline Shreeve is a small but excellent guide to the whole subject.

You Can Heal Your Life by Louise L Hay is an extremely good guide to dealing with problems in your life, based on two fundamental principles – first, that you have to love yourself before you can give and receive love, and secondly, that how events affect you depend entirely on how you think about them.

The Road Less Travelled by M Scott Peck is another very sound guide, based on the four principles of delayed gratification, acceptance of responsibility, dedication to truth and balancing.

A Return to Love by Marianne Williamson is quite religious in bias, but the chapter on relationships is very much worth reading.

Pretty grim, eh? Wouldn't wish depression that bad on my worst enemy. Not that I have one.

The good news, though, is that no matter how bad life gets for you, you can not only get better, but be happy again and stay that way, at least most of the time. It just takes a few simple rules, so let's start with those.

Do what you love

In other words, have a really good think about what it is you love doing most, then find some way of doing it at least some of the time.

With endless perseverance and a bit of luck, if you want something badly enough, you'll find a way to do it.

And I mean endless. Take authors, for example. John Irving, the American author of The World According to Garp, The Hotel New Hampshire and 11 other bestsellers, said he decided to write because he realised that doing anything else would always be vaguely dissatisfying.

And who wants to spend their lives being vaguely dissatisfied?

However, when I say endless perseverance, I mean endless.

A few years ago, The Independent ran a story about the world's most popular authors. Every single one of them had been rejected dozens, if not hundreds of times, before they finally got a book accepted.

Oh, and that old Chinese saying about falling down seven times and getting up eight? What a load of bollocks. You can't get up more times than you fall down. Seven is quite enough, thank you very much.

And while I'm on the subject of old Chinese sayings, don't believe that other one about a man who loves what he does not working a day in his life.

Richard Branson didn't get to be worth squillions by not working a day in his life.

You still need the endless perseverance, but at least if it's endless perseverance at something you love, you wake up every morning looking forward to the challenge.

Live in the moment. It's all you've got

In other words, regretting the past and worrying about the future is just ruining the present.

As Lao Tzu, the founder of Taoism, put it, if you're depressed, you're living in the past, if you're anxious, you're living in the future, and if you're at peace, you're living in the present.

Living in the moment is one of the great rules of life. It gets rid of a load of problems and makes everything instantly more enjoyable. You start to notice everything around you and enjoy, rather than walking around half asleep with your head down, fretting about that time you told your ex that dress didn't actually suit her, or worrying if it's going to snow this Christmas.

And living in the moment makes you a great listener, since you're actually paying attention and learning something. It's why you have two ears and only one mouth.

The book Men are from Mars, Women are from Venus has a great example of how not listening can end up in what Leonard Cohen called the homicidal bitching that goes on in every kitchen:

The wife is talking about a problem she's having. Her husband goes quiet because he's thinking of solutions to her problem. She gets annoyed because she thinks he's not listening. He gets annoyed because he's trying to solve her problem and she doesn't appreciate it. She gets really annoyed because she doesn't want him to solve her problem. She just wants him to listen to show he cares. He gets really, really annoyed because he does care. That's why he was trying to think of a solution.

He decides to go off and become a Zen Buddhist monk and live in a stone hut on top of Mount Fuji in the rain.

She decides to become a lesbian and cover herself in chocolate.

It would all have been so much simpler if he'd just listened.

Here's a little story from my own life about how it's far easier in life to be a headless chicken than to be a Buddha.

After a day spent rushing around doing things, you rush from work to the shops, rush around the shops, fit in a visit to your mother in hospital, rush home and cook, listen to some music with the CD player on fast forward to save time, then brush your teeth quickly, go to bed and fall fast asleep. See? Even sleep doesn't get a chance to be slow.

In none of this do you leave time to sit down for a while and talk to the love of your life. And even if you do, it can all end in tears.

For if you haven't talked properly for weeks, both of you have been germinating little problems which have grown into monsters, and when you finally do sit down to talk about them, they burst out all at once as a many-headed Hydra.

Then something else happens which makes it even worse. If you've ever read Men are from Mars, Women are from Venus, you may remember laughing with recognition about the different way that men and women communicate.

Put bluntly, it says that men are more likely to do, and women to be.

So men are out doing all day, whether it's wrestling bears, shooting down Messerschmitts or finding out how to get the central heating working again. They might have a problem with all of that, but they're convinced they can work it out by themselves.

Now, women are out working and doing as well, but if they have a problem, they're much more likely to phone up their girlfriends and talk about it.

However, what they'd really like to do is go home in the evening, sit down with the love of their life and talk about it more.

So they do. Except the love of their life has been out and about all day doing things, which he feels is his contribution to the relationship.

He comes home, and maybe it's his turn to cook dinner, which is fine, even if he's a bit knackered, because it's more doing, so that's his contribution.

So they sit down over dinner, and he's thinking: great - food, wine and there's a programme about Spitfires on the History Channel in 15 minutes.

And she's thinking: great - at last a chance to sit down and talk.

So she brings out the many-headed Hydra of all the little problems that have been building up into monsters over the past few weeks.

And all he hears is the first one, then goes off inside his head and starts trying to work out the solution to that one. After a while he comes up with one, and presents that to her.

And she thinks: he hasn't even been listening to me. For the last five minutes he's had that faraway look which shows he's been thinking about something else.

And he thinks: here I am, working hard all day doing stuff, then I come home and cook the dinner, and I don't get any thanks for all that. And then when I think of a solution to the problem she's given me, she just comes up with other ones. And that programme about Spitfires started 10 minutes ago.

So he's thinking: I love her, but she doesn't appreciate me. And she's thinking: I love him, but he doesn't listen to me.

Praise the Lord, then, that I am with someone who has the wisdom to regularly sit me down, slap me around the head with a wet kipper, and tell me to stop running around like a headless chicken and just listen.

Sorry about that last sentence. I just needed a late entry for the Mixed Metaphor of the Year Award, and the deadline is tomorrow.

Anyway, to get to that little story I mentioned: last weekend we turned off the TV, lit the fire, put on some low jazz and talked. A lot. About life and love, childhood and adulthood, hopes and fears, memories and the moments that had formed us.

It was great. Far better than the most exciting film, the most emotive piece of music, the most mouthwatering food or the finest wine.

On Saturday, we went for a potter around the transport bit of the Ulster Folk and Transport Museum, looking at old motorbikes and cars, laughing at the fact that the Fintona Horse Tram had several horses over the years, all called Dick, and thinking that the museum should really update its entry on Joey Dunlop, which describes the late ace as alive and well.

Then, rather than cook as we usually do, we took a spin over to Marks & Spencer and bought a bunch of prepared meals as a little treat.

We had them at home in front of the fire: smoked salmon on granary bread, washed down with Chablis, then steak and mushroom pie with buttered and salted potatoes and garden peas, accompanied by a nice Rioja. And apple crumble with custard so thick it refused to come out of the jug.

We were good to ourselves, and why not.

On the Sunday, I'd planned to get back to some doing: cleaning the house, then finishing off varnishing the 486 doors which come with having a grand Victorian Tine Hise. You have to pronounce that way, to give a grand old house the respect it deserves.

I was just getting out the vacuum cleaner when my sister and several friends arrived around, and that was the end of that.

By the time we'd given them tea and buns and had more talking - it was obviously the weekend for it - it was the beginning of twilight, so instead of all the things I'd been planning to do, I did just one: went out the back and chopped some firewood.

And, straightening once, looked in through the great arched wood and glass door we had built, into the warm space of the kitchen, with its lamplight spilling out, its birch and beech wood, its pale yellow walls and the indigo pillar by the range, its giant steel fridge and the row of cookbooks above the old range.

It looked wonderfully welcoming. It looked like home, and for the first time since we had moved in, I appreciated it.

I carried the wood in for the fire, and thought that it had been the simplest of weekends, and the best.

I had remembered that happiness is, rather than doing 10 things badly, doing one thing well, even if it is only chopping wood.

And I had remembered what it is to stop doing, and be, and just listen.

Two phrases you'll never need again

If only...
Should have...

The truth is that you did the best with the knowledge you had. So let it go.

Here's another one you can bin: what if...

How to stop worrying about the future

What are we actually worrying about?

As WE Johns, the author of the Biggles books, put it:

Of two things, one thing is certain:
Either you are on the ground or in the air.
If you are on the ground, there is no need to worry.

If you are in the air, one of two things is certain:
Either you are flying straight or you are turning over.
If you are flying straight, there is no need to worry.

If you are turning over, one of two things is certain:
Either you will crash or you will not crash.
If you do not crash, there is no need to worry.

If you do crash, one of two things is certain:
Either you will be injured or you will not be injured.
If you are not injured, there is no need to worry.

If you are injured, one of two things is certain:
Either you will recover or you will die.
If you recover, there is no need to worry.
If you die, you can't worry.

Think about things you worried about. How many of them came to pass? Not many, I bet.

As Mark Twain said: "I've lived through some terrible things in my life, some of which actually happened."

And if they did happen, were they as bad as you thought they were going to be? Bet they weren't.
So here's the lesson. Stop worrying. All worrying does is make you worried. It doesn't improve the present, and it doesn't change the future.
Not only that, but the things you worry about rarely happen, and if they do, they're rarely as bad as you thought they were going to be.

And remember: courage is not absence of fear, but going ahead in the presence of fear. So be afraid, and do it anyway. Afterwards, you'll have the warm glow of thinking: Well, I was afraid, I did it anyway, it wasn't as bad as I thought, and I feel a lot better for conquering my fear and doing it.
After all, as Mark Twain said – yes, the same one; he said a lot of good things - in 20 years you'll regret the things you didn't do, not the things you did.
Having said that, if at first you don't succeed, do give up skydiving.
I know. I was that man. Still, at least I only twisted my knee.

Here are some other things I did that scared the bejaysus out of me:

Sitting on a motorbike in Delhi, having only done my test two years before, and having only ridden 30 miles in my life, including 20 to the test and back, about to ride the 7,000 miles back to the UK on some of the most dangerous roads in the world, and through countries in which the Foreign Office had told me I would be almost certainly kidnapped and shot.

Flying an aeroplane solo for the first time, and realising the moment that the aircraft left the ground that I was the only person who could get it back down again.

Am I still alive to tell the tale about both of those? Absolutely. And how did I feel after I did them? Great. Thanks for asking.

Staying in the moment: how to do it

Take up something extreme which forces you to give your complete attention to it or die, such as motorcycling, flying, skiing, wrestling crocodiles or correcting your wife when she has PMT.

There are several disadvantages to this method.

It can be expensive.

You can die.

You can only do it some of the time.

Another method is meditation, which is simply a process of sitting still and emptying your mind. As a friend of mine said, it's better than sitting around doing nothing. Quite.

Samurai thought this was great as a prelude for getting in touch with the nothingness at the centre of their being, creating a stillness and purity which meant that they could then go out and kill peasants in a state of exquisite perfection.

However, this is not mandatory. Which is good news for peasants.

If you want, you can prepare for mediation by getting in touch with your senses one by one: make sure you won't be disturbed, then sit in a quiet room.

Feel the weight of your body on the chair, the clothes on your skin, the air on your face and hands, the distant sounds and then sounds closer still, like the sound of breathing.

It's trickier than it sounds, since those pesky thoughts about the past and the future keep butting in.

The answer is not to fight them, but to just let them go without judgement and return to the present.

If it helps, you can focus on a mantra, that is a word repeated over and over, or simply the sound of your own breathing.

The only disadvantages I've found to meditation is that I tend to nod off, and that although the calming effects last for a while, you still have to apply the principle of returning to the present to your everyday life.

And just one last point before we leave the subject of living in the moment by letting go of regret about the past and worry about the future.

It's not something you'll do once and then forget about.

It's something you'll do dozens or hundreds of times a day. You see, regretting and worrying is a habit, and like all habits, it'll keep coming back and knocking on the door of your mind to be let in. Persistent little buggers, habits.

So every time they come knocking, don't panic. Just let them go and come back to the present. Again and again. After a while, they'll call by less often, and when they do come around, they'll just look in the window, see you sitting in a sunny room with a smile on your face, and bugger off to annoy someone else.

OK, I've tried all that and I'm still a bit afraid when something important comes up. What now?

Don't panic. A little fear is a good thing
Sports psychologists say stress improves performance up to a certain point, then ruins it very quickly.

Here's what I used to say when I used to coach the national volleyball squad:
If you're about to hit the ball and you're thinking of what you got up with your better half last night with a feather duster, a bouncy castle and a bottle of baby oil, the ball's pretty safe from being hit properly.
Even if you're thinking of the result of the season, the match, the set, the rally or you hitting the ball, you're not giving your full attention to hitting the ball.
So it's simple. Just stay in the present, and hit the ball.
Again, it's just giving your full attention to the moment, rather than regretting the past and worrying about the future.
I also read some very good advice recently from a psychiatrist who said that fear and excitement are just actually pretty similar; it's just that one is negative, and the other positive.
So the next time you feel fear, just pretend it's excitement.
After I read that, I tried it the next time I was driving to the flying club where I fly a microlight.

I hadn't flown for a while, and as always, I was filled with a niggling fear that I'd forgotten how to do it, so I pretended instead that I was excited about going flying.

And lo and behold, it worked. Now even if I haven't flown for a while, I drive to the airfield feeling excited rather than fearful, and therefore looking forward to it rather than worrying needlessly about it.

So I shouldn't care about what's going to go wrong?

Now you're getting it.

Here's another example from sport. I was an international volleyball player for years, and I've lost count of the number of times I walked back to serve in front of a noisy crowd with the score at match point and my heart making like a Buddy Rich drum solo as I tried to relax and focus on a killer serve.

I dealt with it in a couple of ways. First of all, I thought: we'll all be dead in 50 years, so none of this matters.

Then I looked at where I planned to serve and visualised the ball going there.

And then I tossed the ball, looked at the centre of it, hit it there, and finished my follow through where I wanted it to go. Simple.

When I turned to coaching, I forgot about the being dead in 50 years bit, because I didn't want the team to think I was weird or anything.

But I did tell them when they were serving at those high-stress match points that it was just a drill. That stopped them caring, and when they stopped caring about the result, that meant they were just hitting the ball.

For here's an old Chinese saying that actually makes sense:

When an archer aims at a target, he hits the target.

When you tell him you will give him a bag of gold for hitting the target, he thinks about the pot of gold, and misses the target.

So stop caring about success, and ironically, you're more likely to focus on the job in hand and succeed.

And make this your resolution, not just at New Year, but all day and every day: live in the moment, and have no fear.

OK, I'll sleep on it. Or I would, if I didn't lie awake at four in the morning worrying about stuff

You're not alone. We've all lain awake at four in the morning worrying. And I bet none of us have actually solved the problem at four in the morning.

Four in the morning is for sleeping. Er, unless you're a bus driver on night shift.

That's easy for you to say, but the harder I try to get back to sleep, the harder it is to get back to sleep

Ah yes, that old paradox. Funny enough, it's a bit like the happiness and love we were talking about at the start. The harder you struggle to get them, the less likely you are to succeed.

So stop struggling. Give up. Take a deep breath and let all your muscles go slack. I bet you didn't even realise they were tense.

Now just listen to your breathing. If worries and thoughts arise, don't fight them. That just raises your adrenalin level, makes you tense and defeats the purpose.

Just let them go and listen to your breathing again.

What about speaking in public? Even the thought of it brings me out in a cold sweat and hot flushes at four in the afternoon, never mind the morning

First of all, turn off the electric blanket. And grab your half of the duvet back. That should cure those symptoms.

I used to run a public speaking course for an organisation called Mightier Than The Sword, and the simplest and most practical hints on that are to slow down, to pause more than you think you need to, and to listen to the sound of your own voice.

All of that makes people pay attention and helps you enjoy the whole experience instead of sounding like

Mickey Mouse on helium as you speak faster and faster to get it over as soon as possible.

And remember, you have the power to choose whether you enjoy the experience or not. Do you really want to choose to make it miserable? Of course not. Choose to enjoy it!

OK, I don't have to speak in public too much anyway, so what about everyday stuff? What about multi-tasking? Is it a better way to get more done?

Nope. All multi-tasking means is trying to do several things at the same time, doing them all badly, and getting to the end of the day frazzled and dissatisfied.

In fact, neuroscientists now say that it's actually impossible for your mind to do several things at the same time. What actually happens is that leaps from one thing to another then back again, giving none of them the attention they deserve.

So do one thing at a time, give your full attention to it, then pause, take a deep breath, and give your full attention to something else.

It makes everything a pleasure, from painting a wall to listening to music.

And while I'm on the subject, take the time to do things properly. There are fewer greater pleasures in life than being completely absorbed in something you're doing with no rush to finish it.

That's easy for you to say. I've got this project to finish by yesterday

OK, when you've finished, make a nice cup of tea, sit down and let's talk about time management.

The first thing is to buy a diary, either a digital one or a nice proper analogue one made of paper. I use an A4 daybook as well for longer thoughts.

Make a list of all the stuff you have to do, and prioritise it.

Now here's the clever bit. Sub-prioritise it into stuff that's urgent but not important, and stuff that's important but not urgent.

Like what?

Well, if you're dying to go to the loo, that may not be important, but it's pretty urgent.

If you've a big project to finish by the end of next week, clear a whole day early next week to give yourself the time to do it properly.

OK, but I still feel overwhelmed when I'm faced with a really big project

We all do. The answer is to break it down into a series of smaller tasks, then prioritise them as above.

It's also sometimes a good idea to do the tough bits first so you can relax and enjoy the rest, rather than do the easy bits first and not enjoy them because you're worrying about the harder tasks. Not that you'll worry if you're living in the moment, of course.

It's the same principle as work first, play later. You can also take account of your own preferences: if you're at the best in the afternoons, aim to do the tough stuff then.

What if I don't get to the end of the list?

Doesn't matter. That's the least important stuff, so forget it. Look on the bright side. As I said earlier, we'll all be dead in 50 years, and none of this will matter.

If I just live in the moment, won't it make me deep down a really shallow person? Or a goldfish? Or a goldfish? Or a goldfish?

Yes, yes, very funny. Don't knock goldfish. They might like a bit baffled, but have you ever seen an unhappy one?

You see, you can learn from the past and plan for the future while staying in the present.

For example, in the present you can give your full attention to something you've done in the past; why you did it, how you felt when you were doing it and what the result was.

That way you can use the experience of the past to avoid making the same mistakes in the future. Or, even better, learn from others; as Otto von Bismarck wrote: "A fool learns from his mistakes, but a truly wise man learns from the mistakes of others."

You can also stay in the present while giving your full attention to plans for the future.

Both of these are useful. What's useless are random, pointless regrets about the past, and random, equally pointless anxieties about the future.

What if you're planning for the future, but you're not quite sure which action to take?

Here's a handy hint. Sit down and be still for a few moments. Now think back to something you did in the past which was right and good, then see how that makes you feel. I imagine it'll give you what Australians call the warm fuzzies; a nice, comfortable feeling of wellbeing.

Now think of something that you did that was wrong, and ended badly, and see what feeling arises. I imagine a tense knot of fear somewhere down near your stomach.

Now be still for a few moments more, and think of the first option in your future. See what feeling arises. Then let that go, and think of the second option, and see which feeling arises.

Whichever action makes you feel warm, happy and content is the right one.

OK, that living in the present idea is all very well, but what if the present's crap?

Good question. Let's look at some crap.

Your wife runs off with the postman. Who's hurting? You. They're not.

Running late, you walk into the bank at five minutes to closing time on Friday and find a queue longer than the Great Wall of China. And slower.

Who's annoyed? Just you.

OK, smartass, what's the solution?

Well, don't thank me for this one.

Thank the Stoic philosopher Epictetus, who said that rage, depression, anger and fear only arose when we tried to control things which were outside our control.

He and the rest of the Stoics felt that all we really have control over are our own emotions, beliefs and actions.

Or psychiatrist Viktor Frankl, who woke up in Auschwitz one day and had the epiphany that the Nazis could do what they liked to him, but they couldn't get inside his head unless he let them.

Or Ulric Neisser, whose 1967 book Cognitive Psychology was the basis for modern, er, cognitive psychology.

The basis of it is very simple: it's not what happens to you, but how you react to it that matters.

And here's the best bit of all. You have the power to control how you react to things. Let me say that again, because it's important. You have the power. To choose not only how you react to things, but to be happy, to be positive, to be optimistic, to do good.

In those four words, you stop becoming a victim, tossed and battered by the storms of life, but the master of your own state of mind.

Scary and exciting, isn't it?

You see, as that gloomy bugger Hamlet said, nothing is either good or bad but thinking makes it so.

The trouble was that he never put it into practice, but he was right: happiness or sadness is all in your head, but the good news is it's your head, so it's up to you what you do with it.

And remember, it's your choice. As that slightly less gloomy bugger the Dalai Lama said: "Choose to be optimistic. It feels better."

Great chap, the Dalai Lama. I met him once with a bunch of other journalists, and one of them asked him a very long and very complicated question about the situation in Northern Ireland.

A politician would have produced an answer which left no one any the wiser, but the Dalai Lama just thought for a moment, said: "I don't know", then burst out laughing.

As we all did. Even the person who'd asked the question in the first place.

Yes, yes, that's all very well, but in the meantime, my wife's still run off with the postman, and I'm still stuck in this queue in the bank

Accept what you can't change, change what you can't accept, and have the sense to know the difference. It may be a cliché, but how do you think clichés got to be clichés? By being true, that's how.

Let's take a look at those examples above.
The easy one is the queue in the bank. You can't do anything much about it at that moment, so there's no point getting annoyed about it. Look out of the window. Talk to the next person in the queue. Think of something happy. Make a mental note to have a word with the manager next week about maybe putting more staff on for Fridays. And make a mental note to yourself that if you have to go to the bank on Fridays, get there earlier.

That was the easy one. Now let's take your wife running off with the postman.
You'll go through the classic five stages of grief spelled out by psychiatrist Elisabeth Kübler-Ross back in the Sixties: denial, anger, bargaining, depression and acceptance.

It's only when you get to the last one that it will all start to make sense, when you realise that when someone has locked the door to your heart and walked away, there is little point wasting your life by keeping a candle lit in the window of that heart for a day when they bring back the key and open the door.

In any case, the heart is a wonderful thing: no matter how much it is broken, in time it heals and is ready to love again, and then, of course, you realise that you had been holding the key all along. And that only a true fool loves someone who does not return that singular blessing.

So I shouldn't concern myself with the state of the world? Isn't that, like, opting out, dude?

No, it's just common sense. What's the point of getting angry about the way Robert Mugabe ruined Zimbabwe when you haven't got his phone number to give him a good talking to?
Getting angry about things you can't change just turns you into a Daily Mail reader. Or the bloke in the pub who says: "I make all the important decisions in our house, like whether there's life on other planets, whether Elvis is still alive and whether we should have invaded

Iraq, and my wife makes all the small ones, like where we live, what we eat and where the kids go to school."

So how do I know what can I change?

Depends. If you're the US President, quite a lot. If you're a beggar in the street in Delhi, maybe not so much.

In truth, all you can change is yourself and the way you think and act, but in terms of changing the world, what you can do is do good within your sphere of influence, even if that means doing something positive with every small deed of your day. Tell the girl in the shop that her hair's lovely. Open the door for the old lady. Smile at strangers. Commit small acts of random kindness.

At the end of the day, you will have become the god of small deeds, and created an entire pantheon of diminutive divinities. In fact, if you turn off the light and look out the window, you'll probably see little pinpricks of wellbeing glowing all over the city.

But surely doing good to make yourself feel better is just selfish?

Listen, if we start the old philosophical debate about whether true altruism actually exists, we'll be here until the cows come home. If cows actually exist, that is.

In a way, it doesn't really matter, as long as good gets done, although it's worth noting that my philosophy tutor at university did say to me once that there are three levels of doing good: to make you feel good, to make others feel good, and simply to do good.

Then he went off to become a long-distance lorry driver.

What if I do good and other people are horrible back?

The good news is they mostly won't be.

If they are, first of all it's their problem, and secondly, given the choice, wouldn't you rather be pleasant you than horrible them?

Silly me, I almost forgot: you have the choice.

So I should keep on being nice to people even if they're raving psychopaths back to me?

Funny, I think I went out with her for a while as well.

Up to a point is the answer. Life's too short to spend it in the company of emotional black holes, so if after a few attempts of being nice to someone with no success, walk away. If you're working with them, spend as little time with them as possible. If you're in a relationship with them, er, why?

Er, because any relationship is better than none. And because I'm afraid of being lonely.

Ah yes, the oldest problem in the book: living your life in fear rather than love. Remember what Mark Twain said about regretting the things you don't do rather than the things you do? Think of how you'll feel after 20 years of living with the wrong person rather than having the courage to follow your heart.

And if you are in any doubt about what decision to take, remember that little exercise of sitting down, thinking of one option and seeing what feelings arise, then the other.

But isn't all this self-help stuff just a pathetic excuse for failure? I mean, if I was rich and successful, I wouldn't need it, would I?

I wouldn't bet on it. I met Richard Branson once, and all he did was moan about how he wasn't as rich as Bill Gates.

Oh, all right, he didn't really.

But I was talking to a luxury yacht salesman recently who said Roman Abramovich was a paranoid, miserable git; particularly since his 533ft private yacht had just been overtaken as the longest in the world by Sheikh Khalifa bin Zayed al-Nayan's 590ft one.

And here's the most stupid thing of all: they're both too big to be parked anywhere. That's a technical term, but it means they have to anchor miles from all the best parties, although if you're a paranoid, miserable git, you probably don't get invited to many parties anyway.

You see, no matter how rich you are, or how long your yacht is, there'll always be someone richer and with a bigger one.

I'll come back to this later, but happiness doesn't come from money and things; it comes from passion and people. The next time you're on the interweb, Google Professor Randy Pausch for an inspirational talk from a man who knew he was dying from cancer and wanted to pass on what he'd learned was truly worthwhile.

Talking of dying, what about growing old gracefully? The older I get, the more I find myself pining for my lost youth.

It's easy to do. As Leonard Cohen said: "Sometimes when I am lonely, I get to thinking of the past."

And before you accuse Lennie of being a miserable git, I met him years ago and he told me everyone says that about him, but he was happy once. It was a Thursday.

Wishing you were young again is pointless. Unless you've got a time machine in the garage you're not telling me about.

So live every day to the full, as in the previous section, but accept that one day you're going to go from James Bond to Q. Bernard Llewellyn, that is, not Ben Wishaw.

Of course, when we're young we're filled with a glorious sense of infinite possibilities, and as time goes on, that sense diminishes because we have more past behind us than we have future in front of us; but then that too is a lesson in one of the fundamentals of cognitive psychology that I mentioned - that it's not what happens to you, but how you react to it that matters, and best of all, that we have control over that reaction.

I did say that before, but it's worth repeating.

That, and accepting what is. That you may not make the next Olympics after all. Unless you buy a ticket in the stands.

I know what I'm talking about. Last night I drank too much wine and tried to do 30 press-ups in the bathroom. It hurt.

It was George Bernard Shaw who said that the reasonable man adapts himself to the world, and the unreasonable man tries to adapt the world to him.

That may well mean, as Shaw said, that all progress depends on the unreasonable man, but I suspect that the reasonable man is the happier one.

And I suspect that it may be closer to the truth to say that many of us spend the first half of our lives trying to change the world, and the second half trying to change ourselves.

Here's a hint: the second bit is easier.

So adventure before dementia? I saw that once on a T-shirt in Oz

I like it. Staying young is all in your head. Even if your knees tell you different.

Look at people like Sir Ranulph Fiennes or Michael Palin, who are still going strong.

So get out there and get physical. Even a walk makes you feel better after. I'm 65 and I still play tennis twice a week, and even if my knees moan a bit afterwards, I feel better afterwards.

And thirsty.
But don't drink too much. After one glass, everything is possible. After two or three, nothing is.
It's not for nothing that Dorothy Parker said:
I always have one martini,
two at the very most.
After three I'm under the table,
after four I'm under the host.

And if you do find yourself slipping into that middle-aged, middle class habit of getting through a bottle of wine a night then waking up next morning filled with self-loathing, a good rule is that you can drink as much as you like, but make sure you enjoy every mouthful.

That slows you down and makes sure you actually enjoy the journey rather than hurtling towards the destination of getting sozzled.

But don't fret too much about it: the French enjoy their wine more than anyone, but they eat three good meals a day rather than snacking on fast food, and only about one in 10 is obese compared to a third of Americans.

Talking of enjoying a drink or two, I enjoy my food a bit too much as well, and I've tried every diet going to no avail. Should I just accept that I was born cuddly?

I feel your pain. I joined Heightwatchers last Christmas to try and shed those stubborn extra inches, but I'm still 6ft 7ins and a bit.

The same hint works for food as drink: you can eat as much as you like, but make sure you taste and enjoy every mouthful.

And at no extra charge, here's the only diet that works: eat less, exercise more. Or exercise even more, and eat all you want!

Stuff. It's just stuff.

We all tend to define ourselves in terms of our stuff. Men look at their house, their car, their motorbike or their unique collection of Seventies Japanese pop singles, and they think: this is me. Women stand in front of a crammed wardrobe and say: "But I haven't got a thing to wear!"

The good thing about stuff is that it's great. For a while. You get the BMW 3-series. Then you want the 5. Then the 6. Then the M-series. Then you see the fat, geeky bloke who was in your class at school driving past in a Porsche 911, and in that moment your entire life becomes a complete, miserable failure.

It's not, of course. But it feels like that because you've defined yourself in terms of stuff.

What's the answer? I go on motorbike adventures. You can take so little stuff on a motorbike that it makes you realise you need very little stuff to have an amazing life.

When I spent a month riding Route 66 on a Harley, for example, I just took hand baggage. And even for several months riding around the world, just two T-shirts, pants and socks. Every night when I got in, I'd wash one and change into the other.

And while it's possible to do that for your whole life, like my mates Adam Lewis, Simon and Lisa Thomas and Nick Sanders, it may not even be practical, or even advisable, for you to suddenly announce to your better half over the cornflakes one morning: "Right dear, I'm off for six months to de-stuff myself. Geoff told me to. Here's his number if you want to talk to him about it."

They may well tell you to get stuffed, which would quite defeat the purpose.

No, the simpler answer is to enjoy stuff, but don't define yourself by it. And don't get too attached to it.

As my mate Nick said to me recently, he was clearing his dad's house after he died, and as he was making his umpteenth trip to the skip outside the house, he suddenly thought: "What's the point of all this stuff?"

It was what James Joyce called an epiphany, Ingmar Bergman a wild strawberry moment and Woody Allen a stardust memory.

So stuff only makes us happy for a while. The things that make us happy for ever never change: good friends, good food, good wine, a single flower in a simple room, and when we step out of that room to go walking into the world with the sun on our face and the wind in our hair.

Everything else is just stuff.

Meanwhile, somewhere in Azerbaijan...

Amazon tells me that How to be Happy is too short for a print book, so as a bonus, here's my favourite chapter from Where was I again?, my collected travel stories.

No charge, since it's you.

Azerbaijan: a short history

Fourth Century BC, just after breakfast

Country named Media Atropatene after ruler of area under Alexander the Great.

Fourth Century BC, teatime

Alexander dies. Persians rename country Aturpatakan as part of Caucasian Albania, not to be confused with Balkan Albania, home of Mother Teresa and King Zog.

Fifth Century AD

Arabs conquer and rename country Arran, not to be confused with Scottish island, home of damp sheep.

Treaty of Endless Peace signed.

Sixth Century AD

Endless Peace ends. Endless War begins between Romans, Arabs, Turks, Mongols and Tartars over control of country.

1828

When rest not looking, Russians grab northern half and rename it Азербайджан. Persians grab south, followed by much enraged carpet-thrashing after Russians discover huge quantities of oil in north.

1900

Country producing half the world's oil, and 95 per cent of Tsarist Russia's. Baku becomes Paris of Caucasus. As opposed to France. Or Texas.

1917

Tsars go out in Russia. In Baku, independence declared, women given vote, Latin alphabet adopted and country renamed Azerbaycan.

1920

Russians check national oil gauge, discover they're running on empty, invade country for refill and change language back to Cyrillic.

1980s

Good news: even huger huge oil and gas deposits discovered off coast. Coincidentally, Western governments suddenly become interested in country.

Bad news: war with Armenia over Nagorno-Karabakh creates refugee crisis.

1991

Country becomes independent and decided to call itself Azerbaijan just for a change. Natives, uncertain whether to celebrate in Albanian, Scottish, Persian, Arabic, Russian or Latin for fear of starting another war, hug each other in mute optimism.

1994

So-called Deal of the Century signed with international consortium for exploitation of oil and gas fields.

2003

Respected president Heydar Aliyev hands over power to son Ilham with dying breath.

CIA verdict on Ilham, notorious former playboy converted to family life, is: "Lacks his father's charisma, political skills, contacts, experience, stature, intelligence and authority. Aside from that, he will make a wonderful president." Azerbaijanis, used to waiting and seeing, wait and see.

Azerbaijan

At first Marco Polo came with bales of silk, his hands aromatic with saffron or shimmering with the shadow of jade. In the lilac evenings he walked by the Caspian Sea and cursed the black mud that ruined his golden slippers.

Then the Zoroastrians came, and lit an eternal flame that lasted longer than they did. Then the Rothschilds and the Nobels, here for the same oil that had ruined Marco Polo's slippers, their fantastical mansions rising from the gloop and suck of ruined forests.

Then Stalin came, and the mansions were divided into a thousand tiny apartments, each one still with fear.

Then the oilmen came again, breaking the stillness with loud voices and the rustle of dollars. A hundred years ago Azerbaijan had produced half the world's oil, and now the world was back looking for the other half.

And then, at last, the tourists came. In 1997 the first of them wrote to the Azerbaijani embassy in London, asking for a tourist visa, and the embassy wrote back asking why. Today, foreigners are still so rare that as you walk past the people blink in amazement. Then try to sell you a carpet.

I arrived in Baku, the capital, in the middle of the night, driving through streets where only the flower shops were open, selling lilies to romantic insomniacs.

The next morning, dawn broke over the medieval quarter to reveal a scene from the hotel window which, apart from McDonald's, Mothercare and the mobile phone shop, had not changed in 400 years.

Along the shore stretched the gloriously lunatic mansions of the 19th Century oil barons, mostly farmers who woke up one morning to find themselves millionaires and immediately sent telegrams to Italy for the first available architect to come at once.

On the hill behind rose a vast Soviet edifice whose countless windows had been teased into Islamic arches, like a shot putter who had discovered eye shadow long after steroids.

I rose, ate a fig for breakfast and wandered through rain-damp streets with the feel of a Paris that had not been washed for half a century, until I came at last to the State Carpet Museum, a monolithic neoclassical pile which smelt of shoe polish. On the grey walls of its many rooms hung thousands of carpets, and in the corner of each room sat a dark, beautiful and utterly bored attendant.

You see, the thing about carpets is that one in a white room is breathtaking, but several thousand on peeling grey walls inevitably results in you being led away suffering from a rug overdose.

What has happened is that a singular Oriental skill has become the victim of the Soviet obsession with quantity, and the result is a fracture that cannot be healed.

But then Azerbaijan has been fractured so many times since it was a crossroads of the Silk Road: by the Persians, by the Mongols, by the Soviets, by war with the Armenians over Nagorno-Karabakh, by the war between the Russian desire for vodka and the Islamic disdain for it, by the gap between the oil-rich and the dirt-poor.

It has even been fractured by the very tool of communication, with two changes of language and three of alphabet - Arabic to Latin, to Cyrillic, and back to Latin - in 80 years.

It is no wonder that the past and the present sit uneasily side by side here, like the grandfather and child of estranged parents.

No wonder that, at any crossroads in Baku, you will see impeccably dressed men from among the one-eighth of the population who are refugees - or the one in two who are unemployed - standing looking in bafflement at a Mercedes taxi on its way to Crescent Beach, an exclusive coastal resort for expatriate oilmen.

Or me inside the Mercedes, looking equally baffled for the same reason: that Azerbaijan's share of Caspian Sea oil reserves is reckoned to be at least £50 billion, but none will find its way into the country until the companies pay off their development costs, and even then much of it may well end up lining the pockets of corrupt politicians, businessmen and their relatives.

At Crescent Beach, I ordered emu.

"I am sorry, sir, but the emu is only served at evening time," said the waiter carefully, conjuring up an image of a flock of emu sitting outside, waiting with fear and trembling for the gleam of a Sabatier at twilight.

When I returned to town in the afternoon, the rain was still falling. In crepuscular carpet shops, negotiations began, faltered and continued over endless cups of tea, until tourists emerged blinking into the drizzle, clutching rolls of wool and silk on which pearls of rain were already beginning to form.

Night fell. To the south of Baku it fell on the abandoned Soviet oilfields, a scene out of Mad Max by way of the Kremlin.

Amid the rusting oil derricks, baffled cows pottered about in pools of oil and ruined water, calling out softly to each other: "Here, Gertrude, am I unleaded or four-star?"

Further south, it fell on a barbed-wire encampment where for the price of a bottle of vodka the guards would let you in to gaze on row upon row of abandoned Soviet tanks glistening dourly in the moonlight.

It fell on Fisherman's Wharf, an expat restaurant where from a waiter with an accent halfway between Baku and Boston I inexplicably found myself ordering a chip butty.

And it fell, at last, on the Chechnyan nightclub where I found myself later. Inside, men who had arrived with unidentifiable bulges under their clothing bought Champagne for women with entirely identifiable bulges under theirs.

I slept in a vodka daze, and the next morning took a rattling minibus north with a guide called Lianna, who had sharp cheekbones and matching opinions.

"We are victims of the Chinese curse, 'May you live in times of change'," she said. "Something is being created, but we do not know what it is yet. The ugly part of all this is that a waiter earns more than a professor, and now you phone friends before you call around to see if they have food on the table. In the Soviet times, everyone was poor, but no one was starving."

She was right. Azerbaijan is fascinating because of the influences that have shaped it in the past, and because at the moment it is going through the turmoil that Marx called dialectic, when one political system becomes another. It is the drama of which epic narratives are made: great to write about, grim to live through.

In the northern suburbs, vast Soviet apartment blocks stood apparently derelict. Until you saw hanging from a balcony a row of white shirts, growing grey in the rain.

A few miles on, in the shadow of a rusting factory, a shepherd sat by a guillotine, waiting for someone who could afford a headless sheep for supper.

On all sides stretched an arid plain which had been forest until refugees chopped down the trees for winter fuel. From time to time there appeared crumbling villages and roadside cafés desperate with longing. Lianna looked out through the window and clutched her silent mobile phone, an icon of a brave new world that was always coming but never came.

It was 100 miles before the dun plain gave way at last to deciduous forest. The earth breathed again, and in the shade of the trees boys in astrakhan hats sold apples, peaches and walnuts.

At Quba, gay lights tinkled on the long road into town, and such had been the unremitting gloom of the landscape earlier that the sight made me quite absurdly happy.

We got lost, and commandeered the services of a local man with gold teeth. A construction engineer until the Soviets left, he had returned to his village to work as an allotment farmer and repair man.

He led us up the green and dripping lanes to a little Albanian fire temple and graveyard. Dating from the Third Century BC, and fabulously engraved, it lay utterly untended in a hilltop field, watched by two querulous ewes.

We climbed back on the bus and bounced through the village street as a man in an immaculate beige suit and white shoes came picking his way through the mud. Behind him, the little houses had tin roofs decorated with doves and deer, and the valley was heavy with peach orchards.

We found a restaurant in which the speciality was chicken curry, and a long time later, since the recipe had obviously involved first catching the chicken, we returned, burping politely, to Baku.

The day's catch of tourists had finished buying carpets and caviar, tut-tutting at the poverty and the corruption and salving their conscience with a generous tip at the little Italian restaurant around the corner, and were returning to hotel rooms which contained little bottles of corporate unguents and copies of the city's not one, but two, English language newspapers.

I threw a bottle of vodka and a toothbrush into a bag and drove to the airport, and an hour later my plane rose into the early evening sky, leaving behind the two lives of Baku.

The life of ambassador's cocktail parties, export beers and dinner with the Johnsons from Texas this Friday.

And the other life. A hundred years ago it was the life of the oil workers who came from all over Russia to live in canvas tents from which they peered out at the oil barons strolling in whispering silks to their fabulous mansions.

Today, the oil barons wear Armani chinos, but the refugees are still the same, looking out from under the rim of their dripping tent now as the plane to London turns west, and trying to imagine what kind of world it is going to.

The plane in which I sit, looking down for one last time at the gleaming curve of Crescent Beach, where twilight is already beginning to fall on the long dark night of the emu.

2001

About the author

Geoff is a critically acclaimed author and award-winning journalist based in Belfast.

In a previous life, he was Ireland's most capped volleyball player and a much younger man.

He's a motorbike columnist for the Daily Mirror and previously the Sunday Times, although his columns are a desperate attempt to disguise the fact that he knows bugger all about motorbikes.

He's also the editor of Microlight Flying magazine, in spite of the fact that he knows even less about aeroplanes than he does about motorbikes.

His 19 books include novels, travel books, collected newspaper columns and bike adventure books about epic journeys from Delhi to the UK, Chile to Alaska and around Australia.

For his latest adventure book, In Clancy's Boots, he recreated the journey of Carl Stearns Clancy, the first person to take a motorbike around the world 100 years ago – complete with the original boots Clancy wore on that trip.

He's either won or been shortlisted for a UK travel writer of the year award nine times. He's also a former

Irish, European and world travel writer of the year, UK feature writer of the year and Northern Ireland features journalist of the year three times.

He lives in Belfast with his wife Cate, a cat called Cat, a hammock and the ghost of a flatulent Great Dane. His hobbies are volleyball, flying, motorbikes, tennis, skiing and worrying about the price of fish.